EVENTIDE

by Barney Norris

SAMUEL FRENCH

samuelfrench.co.uk

FOR AMATEUR PRODUCTION ENQUIRIES

UNITED KINGDOM AND WORLD
EXCLUDING NORTH AMERICA
plays@samuelfrench.co.uk
020 7255 4302/01

Each title is subject to availability from Samuel French,
depending upon country of performance.

THINKING ABOUT PERFORMING A SHOW?

There are thousands of plays and musicals available to perform from Samuel French right now, and applying for a licence is easier and more affordable than you might think

From classic plays to brand new musicals, from monologues to epic dramas, there are shows for everyone.

Plays and musicals are protected by copyright law so if you want to perform them, the first thing you'll need is a licence. This simple process helps support the playwright by ensuring they get paid for their work, and means that you'll have the documents you need to stage the show in public.

Not all our shows are available to perform all the time, so it's important to check and apply for a licence before you start rehearsals or commit to doing the show.

LEARN MORE & FIND THOUSANDS OF SHOWS

Browse our full range of plays and musicals and find out more about how to license a show

www.samuelfrench.co.uk/perform

Talk to the friendly experts in our Licensing team for advice on choosing a show, and help with licensing

plays@samuelfrench.co.uk   020 7387 9373

Acting Editions

BORN TO PERFORM

Playscripts designed from the ground up to work the way you do in rehearsal, performance and study

---

Larger, clearer text for easier reading

Wider margins for notes

Performance features such as character and props lists, sound and lighting cues, and more

---

+ CHOOSE A SIZE AND STYLE TO SUIT YOU

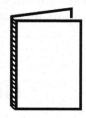

STANDARD EDITION

Our regular paperback book at our regular size

SPIRAL-BOUND EDITION

The same size as the Standard Edition, but with a sturdy, easy-to-fold, easy-to-hold spiral-bound spine

LARGE EDITION

A4 size and spiral bound, with larger text and a blank page for notes opposite every page of text. Perfect for technical and directing use

Other plays by BARNEY NORRIS
published and licensed by Samuel French

Echo's End

While Were Here

FIND PERFECT PLAYS TO PERFORM AT
www.samuelfrench.co.uk/perform

AUTHOR'S NOTE

Eventide was the second full-length play I wrote, and was intended as a celebration of the pub I'd worked in while I was writing my first play, *Visitors*. Getting that show off the ground took an enormous amount of work, and I couldn't have a full time job while I was doing it. So my dad put me up in his spare room in Andover in Hampshire, and for food money I used to cycle out to this pub called The Cricketers in the village of Tangley and work on the bar there a few days a week. Tangley is a precious place to me, a glimpse of a world I feel I come from but can't seem to work out how to live in now. It has a sense of imperviousness about it, a feeling in its steep lanes that it will outlast a lot of the noise that this century is making. Or that was the feeling I got from it, anyway. This play was written out of love, about people I feel very close to, and it's undoubtedly one of my proudest achievements. I wanted to say, in miniature, that the raucous, riotous, poetic spirit of the landscape that produced me may be beset around with dismal stories, and challenged and confounded, but for all that, it is undoubtedly beautiful. It is worth celebrating. It is deeply human, and full of heart. I hope that comes across in the writing.

Eventide was first presented by Up In Arms and Arcola Theatre in association with the North Wall on 25th September 2015, with the following company:

Mark – Hasan Dixon
John – James Doherty
Liz – Ellie Piercy

Director – Alice Hamilton
Designer – James Perkins
Lighting Designer – Simon Gethin Thomas
Sound Designer – George Dennis
Production Manager – Tamsin Rose
Company Stage Manager – Charlie Young
Assistant Stage Manager – Rebecca Denby
Costume Supervisor – Jennie Quirk
Producer – Chloe Courtney
Assistant Director – George Nichols
Marketing and Production Assistant – Rachael Harrison

CHARACTERS

JOHN – a pub landlord
MARK – a young man
LIZ – a village organist

You're pretending this isn't your life. You think it's going to happen some other time. When you're dead you'll realise you were alive now.

Caryl Churchill, *Mad Forest*

ACT ONE

MARK *is sitting with a toolkit. Enter* **JOHN** *with a log basket.*

JOHN Bloke walks into a pub. And he goes to the bar and orders a pint and while he's waiting for it, this feller sidles up to him and says do you wanna buy a ferret? 'Scuse me? Our hero replies. Do you wanna buy a ferret? The feller says again. Not really, says our man. Ah, but this is no ordinary ferret, says the other feller. No no no. This ferret gives the best blow job in the world. You what? Says the first bloke. I'm telling you, says the stranger, I am in possession of a ferret that gives the best blow job in the world. However, it's coming up Christmas and I've got a tax bill to pay, so I need to realise some of my assets, and for that reason I'm willing to let you have this ferret for the ever so reasonable sum of five hundred quid. A monkey for a ferret? Asks the first bloke. Monkey's five hundred quid, Mark, in case you're not as down with the kids as I am. Case you're not street. Where was I? Tell you what, says the other feller, don't just take my word for it. I can see you're the sort of bloke likes to know what he's buying, fair enough. I respect that. I admire it. So why not pop in the gents and give him a test run? And he slips this ferret in the other feller's pocket, and the other feller's not sure what to do, so rather than give it back and risk offence, he goes off to the gents. He's English, see, he doesn't want to say no directly. So he goes in this cubicle, and he's alone with this ferret, and he thinks, this has got to be a practical joke. There's no way I'm letting my cock anywhere near this ferret's teeth. But he's in the cubicle now. He'll feel like an idiot if he comes out without having tried it. And he thinks to himself, wouldn't it be amazing if it was true? Wouldn't it be an amazing thing if there was a ferret who gave the best blow job in the world? And isn't that worth a little risk, a thought like that? So he takes a deep breath, and opens his flies, and five minutes later he's back in the bar with a grin a mile wide, saying he has to get to a cashpoint. So he buys this ferret, and takes it home, and he shows it to his wife. I've bought a ferret, he says. Why? Says the wife. Well this is no ordinary ferret, he says. This ferret gives the best blow job in the world. That's wonderful, says his wife, but what do you want me to do with it? Easy, he says. Teach it to cook and fuck off.

MARK *laughs.*

MARK That's good that is, I like that.

JOHN Mm.

MARK It's got a twist at the—

JOHN Jokes don't want deconstructing, Mark, it spoils 'em. Let it remain as a beautiful snowflake.

MARK Right. Yeah.

JOHN *starts to fill the log basket with firewood.*

Stocking up?

JOHN Mm.

MARK Hot day for a fire.

JOHN Blaze in my grate every day of the year. It's part of what people come for, you know?

MARK Oh yeah.

JOHN Horrible mangy dogs and an unpleasantly hot public bar. That's what I'm selling really. More than the ham, egg and chips. All kinds of places shift food and drink, it's sweat and dogs make me distinctive.

MARK Fair enough.

JOHN She meant a lot to you didn't she.

MARK Not – yeah. She did, yeah.

JOHN I suppose it's not my place.

MARK You're all right.

JOHN Guess you're getting it from everyone.

MARK Not every one's got as big a mouth as you.

JOHN That's my job, isn't it. Ask all the awkward questions. Listen to all the awkward answers. Know all the secrets. That's the art. Innit. Sometimes all your life feels like a falling away of everything from you, don't you think? I think that. And when you get to considering it, it's hard to see the point really, innit. Where was I? You have to carry on though.

MARK No 'have to' about it, far as I see.

JOHN Mm?

MARK Time just keeps fuckin' happenin' to you, don't it. 'Have to' makes it sound like there's a – I dunno, like there's a choice. It's more like – it's like you're on a Megabus, right, or maybe a National Express, I dunno, and you pass a crash on the other side of the motorway, and you want to have a look, you know? But before you can get a proper goosey you're past it, and the road's going on, and you're hurried away from the scene of the accident. Like. Yeah. Because you're headed for Plymouth or wherever, you weren't meant to stop there. That's what absolutely everything is like. Fuck it, anyway. How are you, John, are you all right? It's not a great day for you either is it.

JOHN Today?

MARK What with—

JOHN I know what you're saying. It's not great, no.

MARK What will you do, do you think?

JOHN I don't know. Sit perfectly still. Don't have the energy for anything except a drink.

MARK It's not good, man.

JOHN Not in the long run, no, but I get a certain bitter pleasure from it now. And I don't know what's so wrong with sitting perfectly still. When Chris Marsden announced he was going to retire – you remember Chris Marsden, used to play centre mid for Southampton? – he went on the radio and said his plan was to go to a beach in Greece and just sit there. In the sun. And the interviewer asked him, joking like, don't you think you'll get bored? He just laughed, he said no mate, I think I'll get tanned.

MARK *laughs.*

You ever read W.H. Davies?

MARK Don't think so.

JOHN He was a tramp. And a poet. For a little while he lived in a shed at the bottom of Edward Thomas's garden. Who was a manic depressive. And also a poet, who died in the war. Which is one of the best comedies never written. Not the war, the two poets. And W.H. Davies wrote this poem, 'a poor life this if, full of care, we have no time to stand and stare'. You know that?

MARK *Four Weddings and a Funeral.*

JOHN It was the Center Parcs advert actually, but never mind. What I'm saying is, W.H. Davies, when he was living in Edward Thomas's shed, he wasn't a million miles from here. All in the shadow of the Forest. Same as Chrissy Marsden, see? And I don't think people recognise that there's a distinctive outlook which belongs to this part of the world, which is about sitting around doing fuck all for as long as you possibly can. That's what it's all about, isn't it, pubs and cricket or whatever. Sitting around doing nothing. And people associate that with laziness, but it's not. It's the embodiment of a – of a philosophy. Consider the lily.

MARK What?

JOHN They toil not, neither do they spin.

MARK What?

JOHN Fucking Bible, innit. Bible's full of stuff about not having to work. Parable of the prodigal son's all about that. Don't worry about putting a shift in, fuck off on a jolly and we'll do you a roast.

MARK Yeah, I never get that one.

JOHN Why not?

MARK I don't know why people give more credit to the bloke who fucked off and cocked up then came home than the bloke who stuck around and got on with things.

JOHN I think it's about getting converts.

MARK How?

JOHN Well it was a new religion, wasn't it. Christianity. So it was like a message to say, be nice to floating voters. They'll end up deciding the election.

MARK Right.

JOHN Or something else.

MARK What?

JOHN Well I was just thinking, maybe it's a way of saying, try and do something with your life. Be deliberate, you know?

During your life, try and make one conscious decision. Cos you'll always have where you came from. So you might as well have a go at trying to find something else for as long as you've got a home to come back to, and not just truck along the same furrow for ever.

MARK It'll all get better, you know, John.

JOHN It might get number. I'll give you that. But it'll always have happened, and nothing that's happened to you, really happened to you like that ever gets better, does it. It might get number, I'll give you that. Look at me. I ought to be comforting you.

MARK No—

JOHN You did care for her, didn't you.

MARK It's strange. Cos I did, I can admit that now, I did. Yeah. And I feel – but I've no more right to grieve than anyone else, have I. Cos. No reason to feel any – more than anyone else. And sure, we were close for a while, at school or whatever, yeah, and I loved all that, when we were at school, but not for any real reason, only because we shared a few classes, you know? And I've never had the kind of girlfriend where you're – you know, where you're happy, so I don't know, but I think people who are close like, I mean properly close, like, maybe I mean people who are in love, sort of thing, there must always be more to it than that, mustn't there? Some – feeling you both have, which is more than just sharing a few classes, and you fancying her and her not minding you. Which is more or less. Maybe not for the likes of me, maybe I'll end up taking what I can get or have to stay on my own for ever, or whatever, but for the likes of her, you know? There must be actual love that's like a thing, that exists. Don't you think? So I don't feel more important than anyone else. No. I don't feel I should be, anyway. So it's strange how I'm feeling today.

JOHN How, strange?

MARK Because I loved her, to be honest. Yeah. Yeah. I've never said that to anyone before.

JOHN Not even to her?

MARK Course not. Fuck. Last of all to her.

JOHN But you loved her.

MARK I still do. That doesn't stop, does it.

JOHN No. It just becomes something you can cope with. Or that's what we must both hope.

MARK Sometimes I sort of wish I'd never felt anything in my life.

JOHN I hear that.

MARK Yeah?

JOHN Or I wish things could be undone. Like, if Cath had run over my foot when she drove off, you know, so I could hate her a little bit and undo some of what I actually feel. But she didn't. Well. Wouldn't have worked anyway. You just have to live with the feelings that happen to you, don't you. Everything I ever felt about her is still there. Look at us. I could cry, and I haven't even had my breakfast. Do you want a drink?

MARK I'd better not.

JOHN Let me stand you a beer. You're earning that today. This is my last day as a landlord, let me stand you a beer.

MARK Just a bottle, not a pint.

JOHN All right. I might have one with you.

MARK Don't you need to start prepping lunch, mate?

JOHN In a bit. There's a little while left.

Enter LIZ.

LIZ Morning!

JOHN Hello, Liz, you all right?

LIZ I'm OK, how are you?

JOHN Wanna hear a joke?

LIZ Really?

JOHN Go on, little joke.

LIZ Go on then.

JOHN Bloke walks into a pub. And he goes to the bar and orders a pint and while he's waiting this feller sidles up to him and says, do you wanna buy a ferret? 'Scuse me? Our hero replies. Do you wanna buy a ferret? The feller says again. Not really. Ah, but this is no ordinary ferret, says the other feller. This ferret gives the best blow job in the world. You what? Asks the first bloke. I'm telling you, says the stranger, I am in possession of a ferret that gives the best blow job in the world. However, it's coming up for Christmas and I've got a tax bill to pay, so I'm gonna let you have it for the ever so reasonable sum of five hundred quid. Five hundred quid for a ferret? Asks the first bloke. Tell you what, says the other feller, you don't just have to take my word for it. Why not pop in the gents and give the little feller a test run? And he slips this ferret in the other feller's pocket, and the other feller goes off to the gents, and ten minutes later he's back in the bar with a grin a mile wide, saying he has to get to a cashpoint. So he buys this ferret, and takes it home, and he shows it to his wife. I've bought a ferret, he says. Why? Says the wife. Well this is no ordinary ferret, he says. This ferret gives the best blow job in the world. That's wonderful, says his wife, but what do you want me to do with it? Easy, he says. Teach it to cook and fuck off.

MARK *laughs again.* LIZ *doesn't.*

LIZ You're awful, John, you know that?

JOHN It's a reputation I try to live down to. Lemonade?

LIZ Yes please.

JOHN I'll get it.

LIZ You don't have to—

JOHN Glad to. Don't worry. Always silver service when you come to The White Horse.

LIZ Well. Thanks.

Exit JOHN *with the log basket, which is now full of firewood.* LIZ *lights up.*

Sorry – do you mind if I smoke?

MARK Go ahead.

LIZ This is the smoker's table, isn't it.

MARK I think you can smoke anywhere outside really, but this is where people come, innit, yeah.

LIZ Sort of behind the bikeshed I suppose. Because it feels a bit naughty. Sex sex sex, isn't it.

MARK What?

LIZ Smoking. I don't know where sex stops and smoking begins.

MARK No?

LIZ Cos you start to become sexualised, don't you. When you're growing up, you start to feel – but you don't realise maybe that that's what's happening. Not straight away. All you know is you want to do something – I don't know, you feel – and there's this ban on tobacco advertising, so that must be naughty, right? So maybe you wanna do that. And James Dean's always smoking, and you just know he's shagged every night, and deep down you know it's about getting laid really, you do know, so they sort of get—

MARK Linked in your head.

LIZ That's it! And there's all the – I don't know, there's a sort of phallic aspect, isn't there? Look at that. Of course a penis is bigger than that, in most cases, but all the same. Do you want one?

MARK You're all right.

LIZ Or maybe it's more about nipples, I don't know. Maybe fags are like, a flight from sexuality, maybe it's wanting to get back to sucking on nipples, while you're growing up, after a ride, so you get something to put in your mouth. And it's not a cock, it's a thumb to suck. But on fire. I'm Liz by the way.

MARK Oh. Mark.

LIZ Hi Mark. Sorry, I – mm. Sure you don't want one?

MARK Actually would you mind?

LIZ Course not.

MARK Thanks.

    MARK *lights up.*

LIZ God, I was gasping. I don't like to smoke in the car. I volunteer for Contact the Elderly, do you know them?

MARK Erm—

LIZ They had some very good adverts about two years ago, sort of riffing on *When Harry Met Sally*, do you remember them?

MARK I don't think so.

LIZ Anyway, that was how I heard about them. They're great. Their thing is that older people get very isolated, very alone, so they arrange these tea parties. And you can volunteer either to host one where you live or to drive the elderly people to and from these parties, and stay with them while they're there to make sure they're all right.

MARK Nursery school for old people.

LIZ Yeah, I suppose. Anyway, I live in a shoe box so I can't have people round, but I can drive, so I volunteer for that bit, which I love. But the trouble is it means I don't like to smoke in my car, or it stinks of fags and I worry they'll think I'm degenerate, or choke to death on second-hand smoke. So whenever I get to the end of a drive I'm always gasping.

MARK Right.

LIZ You don't smoke usually?

MARK No. I always thought I'd smoke when I grew up, cos my Dad did—

LIZ Then it killed him?!

MARK It did actually, yeah.

LIZ Oh God, I'm so sorry.

MARK No, but it wasn't that that stopped me.

LIZ No?

MARK It was the smoking ban, really. You know? Cos my idea of smoking couldn't actually come true, like, by the time I started earning enough money to buy any fags. So there didn't seem much point in it. Yeah. There you go, that's how it goes, isn't it.

LIZ Little bit of your cultural inheritance robbed from you.

MARK Yeah.

LIZ Is it true they're putting the war memorial back up today?

MARK What?

LIZ Well I'm playing for this funeral this morning. I'm the organist for the church, you see. And this funeral, it's this girl from round here who drove her car into the war memorial and died last week. So sad. She was back from university and driving too fast, and apparently she didn't have her car with her in London so she hadn't been driving for a few months and she was out of practice and she sort of lost control. It's so sad, isn't it. I don't think they should let such young people on the roads, they can't be trusted. It's a wonder she didn't hurt anyone else. But anyway, the vicar told me when I was parking my car, I always park my car there first then have my fag here and a lemonade to spruce up because I don't like smoking near the church in case Jesus sees me, the vicar said there's actually going to be work being done on the war memorial today, while the bloody hearse goes by! They'll be putting it back together while she gets driven past, how tasteless is that?

MARK Right.

LIZ Did you know her, the girl who died? Are you from round here at all?

*Enter **JOHN** with three drinks.*

JOHN An Englishman, an Irishman, a Scotsman, a Dutchman, a Belgian, a Welsh bloke, a Frenchman, a German, a Spaniard, a Uruguayan, a Brazilian, an American, a Canadian mounted policeman, an Indian, an Australian, a Kiwi, a Peruvian, a Slovenian, a Russian, a Ukrainian and a Chinaman walk up to a nightclub, and the doorman says, sorry gents, you can't come in. Why not? They all ask. The doorman shrugs. Because you haven't got a Thai. Thank God for cheeky beers.

MARK Cheers.

LIZ That was actually much less racist than I expected it to be, John, well done. You can keep that one.

JOHN No, they're like mayflies, jokes. I keep 'em for one day only. After that they're yours to cherish and disseminate or otherwise discard.

LIZ Well I obviously never tell any of them to anyone I know.

JOHN Why not?

LIZ Without being a nun or anything I have sort of constructed a persona that doesn't really leave room for blow job jokes.

JOHN The ferret joke isn't a blow job joke. It's a subversive exploration of the prejudices of its audience.

LIZ Is it.

MARK It's a beautiful snowflake.

JOHN It feints with one overextended comic situation then surprises the listener with a different joke about chauvinist conceptions of women. And in the laughter or the silence it prompts in the listener, which is more genuine and honest thanks to the element of surprise that comes by way of building up the first dummy joke, it invites said listener to learn something about themselves and their own preconceptions.

LIZ It's not, it's a blow-job joke. You're a tosser, John, but I like you for trying to talk your way out. Should you be drinking this early?

JOHN No.

LIZ You will anyway?

JOHN Yup.

LIZ I tell him all the time but I don't think he believes in liver failure, he thinks it's like the tooth fairy or the female orgasm.

JOHN I always start with a cheeky beer about now. Then six or eight of those and then a bit of rosé, maybe a bottle of rosé for the afternoon, then VATs for the evening.

LIZ VATs?

MARK Vodka and tonic.

LIZ Christ, John.

JOHN It's a lot, isn't it.

LIZ It's quite a lot. How many vodka and tonics you drink?

JOHN Sometimes six. Sometimes sixteen.

MARK I suppose you're a big enough bloke like.

LIZ You shouldn't do that to yourself.

JOHN I can hold it. You should stick around some time, you'll find I become quite talkative.

LIZ I find you quite talkative enough.

MARK Do you need so much, to feel it then?

JOHN No, not really. It just helps, is all.

LIZ How?

JOHN Well I think there's some comfort in being able to put your finger on precisely what your problem is, you know? Get your feelings into boxes. If I was just existentially mournful that'd be awful, but because I've got a drinking problem...

LIZ You've arranged yourself a drinking problem so you can have something concrete to feel depressed about?

JOHN Exactly. No, I just like a drink really. And it's all free for me, isn't it. At the point of delivery. My little alcoholic NHS in there.

LIZ Why do you think you're depressed?

JOHN My wife left me.

LIZ Oh John.

JOHN What?

LIZ You tell such terrible—

JOHN No, she—

LIZ Seriously?

JOHN Yeah.

LIZ Is he joking?

MARK Erm—

LIZ John, I'm so sorry.

JOHN Nearly a year ago now.

LIZ Oh fuck. That's why I never see her around any more?

JOHN That'd probably be it.

LIZ I thought she must have lie-ins or something.

JOHN No. Not here anyway. Possibly she has lie-ins in Marlborough with her new antique-dealing boyfriend.

LIZ A year?

JOHN Yeah, been a while now. It's all over really, bar the attention, seeking suicide attempt. Divorce papers an' everythin'. Scrawl on the line. I've written the first fifty thousand words of an agony memoir about it.

LIZ I've come here every month for a year and you've never said anything.

JOHN Well it's not something you bring up, is it, really. And you never come in the pub, they all have a laugh about it in there, but you have your drink out here, and I'm not gonna bring you a lemonade and tell you a thing like that. My wife left me. Sounds like an awful chat-up line. You might think I was trying it on!

LIZ I just feel so awful.

JOHN I bet you do. I've been on the market for a year, you haven't been buyin'. Not that I'd charge, not for you anyway.

LIZ Oh, John.

JOHN What? What?

Silence.

MARK You must get proper fuckin' hangovers drinking that much, right, John?

JOHN I think I'm always just a bit pissed. 'Specially now. What with... It was already happening before she left, that was how I knew she wasn't making it up. She said something about me and the drink when she left. No, that's unfair. She was clearer than that, I'm being unfair. She said I wasn't the man she'd married any more, and I hadn't been for a long time, and this wasn't the life she'd thought we'd have, and it never had been. And she said she'd turned fifty and it'd made her think, and if she didn't do something with her life now, she'd never be able to live with herself. Cos when the day came that her legs stopped working all she'd have to entertain herself with would be this, us, and it wasn't enough for her. And she said she'd decided she was never going to do anything living with me. Then she told me I drank too much. Then she told me she was sorry. Then she told me I ought to look after myself. Then she left. I had to look at myself and say, I suppose you haven't been happy for a long time either. Anyway.

MARK Fuck mate.

JOHN Yeah.

LIZ That's so beautiful.

JOHN What?

LIZ I mean sad. Beautiful and sad. Same thing.

JOHN That's a weird little insight into your head right there.

LIZ Is it?

MARK You getting a decent send-off?

JOHN Not really. People are keeping away.

MARK Why?

LIZ Where are you going?

JOHN Away. I've sold up.

LIZ What?

JOHN Cath wanted her half of everything. Which is her right, and which she's more than earned, I reckon. So I had to sell up. No money for buying her out of the pub.

LIZ Fuck.

JOHN It's all right.

LIZ No, fuck. Are you all right?

JOHN Course.

LIZ Today?

JOHN I know.

MARK Why hasn't anyone been round to say goodbye?

JOHN I don't know mate, do I. I only know they haven't come. I like to think of it as a reminder. Any time I've thought I was anything more than a service to people I've been fooling myself. All I am and ever have been is a supplier of alcoholic products. People don't feel emotional connections to pubs, not really. They say they do, but... They're places to pass through, places to drink in. Or if people do feel emotional connections, it's nothing to do with me.

LIZ There are people who'd say you're the life and soul of the place.

JOHN You might say that. I couldn't possibly comment.

MARK They'll turn up.

JOHN I think maybe once you know something's closing, it starts to look sick. People maybe steer clear of a place once its notice is posted, in case they catch something. Catch closing time, sort of thing. And apart from anything else, I think people are boycotting because I'm selling to the man.

LIZ No.

MARK What man?

JOHN You know.

MARK No.

LIZ The / man the man.

JOHN You know, the "stick it to the man" man! Don't you say that? Maybe that's gone out of fashion. Christ I feel old talking to you. Look, this pub's never been part of a chain before, has it. And I won't feel guilty, cos there just aren't people looking to buy pubs anywhere, but I do feel ashamed in a way. Because a pub's a business, sure, but it's supposed to be more than that, isn't it. It's much more than that. You have responsibilities. To the soul of a place. Because there is such a thing as society. It happens here, I see it every evening.

MARK I wouldn't beat yourself up, mate. It'll still be selling the same drinks, won't it.

LIZ And no one's going to blame you if you didn't have a choice.

JOHN But there are ideas I should be sticking up for. That's what living in the country means. We don't just live here, do we, it's a philosophy, it's an argument we're making.

LIZ Yes exactly. That's exactly what it is, I've always thought that. We believe in long walks and cold showers and early mornings.

JOHN Well—

MARK I don't think that's true.

LIZ No?

MARK I think that's true if you can afford it. If. Far as I see, living here means keeping your head above water. Or fighting to. And failing, and moving to town, and all that breaking your heart. And no money and damp in the bedroom and taking a third or fourth job just to stay where you are, like, cos you only know this life you were born to, don't you, and you don't want to change it. And no, no one's going to bed at night praying for - I don't know, an All You Can

Eat Buffet, but it's not so different from what you do, so I wouldn't feel too bad mate.

LIZ Sorry.

MARK What?

LIZ I'm sorry.

MARK Right.

LIZ I didn't mean to upset you.

MARK I'm not fucking upset.

Silence.

JOHN I like you Marky Mark. You're like me.

MARK Am I?

JOHN We've got things in common, see, Liz, him and me.

LIZ Yeah?

JOHN We've both lost women we love.

LIZ Oh—

MARK Do you think so?

JOHN What?

MARK Do you think we're in the same boat there? Fuck's sake. You had the chance to love her. I just had a few years when I used to know a girl who was too good for me. You had the chance to love her. She'll be too good for me for ever now. I'll never have – well I never will have – well. Fuck's sake.

Silence.

JOHN I'm sorry, Mark.

MARK No, no.

JOHN No, but I am. I'm being—

MARK It's all right.

JOHN You're right. Yeah. I'm sorry. You're right. I didn't have a chance to make her change her mind, though. I had no say in her decision to take away the meaning of my life. Like that. Just like that. I'm gonna go in.

LIZ Stay a minute.

JOHN Why?

LIZ I don't know. I'm just—

JOHN I need to get to work really.

LIZ Are you all right? Will you be all right?

JOHN I'm all right.

LIZ Maybe I'll drop round later. We could talk some more.

JOHN What about?

LIZ I don't know. If you wanted to talk about how you were feeling.

JOHN Oh, right. That's not really something I go in for, to be honest.

LIZ OK. Well the offer's there.

JOHN All right. See you later, Mark.

MARK Yeah all right. I'm sorry, John. I didn't mean—

JOHN I know. You two gonna be all right?

MARK Yeah.

JOHN Liz?

LIZ Me? Yes I'm fine. I ought to be going, really. Don't want to be late.

JOHN I suppose you're not going? To the—

MARK No. Can't, can I.

JOHN All right. I have to start on lunch.

Exit JOHN.

MARK What was that all about?

LIZ What?

MARK Your little rendezvous.

LIZ I just think he might want someone to talk to.

MARK Oh yeah.

LIZ I just think he might need some help, is all. He's a kind man, you know. Under all that. He's not actually a wanker. I don't think. He always brings me my drink. I think he looks after me, you know.

MARK Why do you need looking after?

LIZ No, I don't mean – I don't need that. I don't need anyone to look after me. Is that the funeral you said you couldn't go to?

MARK Yeah.

LIZ You did know her then.

MARK Yeah.

LIZ I'm sorry. I hope I didn't say anything—

MARK No, you're all right.

LIZ Sometimes I talk too much.

MARK It's because of the centenary, innit.

LIZ What?

MARK That's why there's been a rush to get the memorial done. We're having events like everywhere else. Hundred years on sort of thing. Boo hoo. So the council want it fixed quick as poss cos it's supposed to be part of all the events, see? Something to march past. Trouble is, what maybe looks like a sensible decision at council level, the war memorial's fallen down, let's get it back up again sharpish, always looks a bit different to the people on the ground, you're right. What looks efficient on a meeting agenda looks sort of fucking tasteless when she gets driven past the road works, that's true. And the worst of it is that out here, what starts as a council policy always ends up as a local taking a day's work doing something he wishes he didn't have to, cos he doesn't know how else he's going to pay his rent. So yeah, I know quite a lot about the war memorial getting fixed. It's me that's doing it.

LIZ Oh.

MARK I don't want to. She was my best friend. I felt that anyway. She had a lot of friends, but she was *my* best friend. But I have to take the work, see. Round here there's little enough before you start turning stuff down on principle. From the fuckin' council an' all. You don't wanna be on their blacklist.

LIZ I'm so sorry.

MARK I feel so sad about it. Cos she used to let me hold her hand, you know? And I can still feel what that felt like. You know? Yeah.

LIZ I really didn't mean to be rude. I feel awful.

MARK You weren't rude. I'm fuckin' furious about it. But I've been a motorway repairman and slept five nights a week in my cab by the side of the road, I've chipped the mortar off bricks while the snow was falling. You do the work, that's all, you do the work there is and pay the rent and pay the rent. There's no say in it. You ought to go, you know. It won't be long before people start arriving. Fuckin' flowers everywhere I suppose, all round the church.

LIZ Yes. Flowers everywhere. I don't want to leave you like this.

MARK Like what?

LIZ You know. I don't know. Sad.

MARK I don't really think there's anything you can say that's going to do much about that.

LIZ Right. No. Of course. Well perhaps I'll—

MARK He's all right you know, John. If you were looking for a character reference. He's all right.

LIZ It's nothing like that. I just thought he might need a friend, OK?

MARK All right. Just saying. Nice to meet you.

LIZ And you. Perhaps I'll see you later.

MARK Well you'll know where to find me. I'll be putting the memorial back up.

ACT TWO

JOHN is sitting on the bench, a crown on his head, a pewter tankard in his hands. He sits. He looks into the tankard. It's got a glass bottom, and he waves his hand under it then sits up and looks out as if it's a telescope. He cries. Enter LIZ.

JOHN *(sings)*

> AND IT'S NO, NAY, NEVER,
> NO NAY NEVER NO MORE,
> AND I'LL PLAY THE WILD ROVER,
> NO NEVER, NO MORE.

LIZ John?

JOHN Oh. Sorry. I was—

LIZ What's the matter?

JOHN They all turned up.

LIZ Who?

JOHN For the wake of course, they were having the wake here. The whole village. And then—

LIZ What?

JOHN Bill Owen, do you know Bill? Oldest buffer here. Father of the village, if you will. Or he likes to act like he is. Lives along in one of the cottages, he's been there since about forty eight, he's gone ninety. You might not know him, he doesn't go to church. Bill stands up and the place falls silent. The whole village is looking at him. And he says we all know today is a sad day, today is Lucy's day, but there's someone else who's leaving us this evening, and the number of times I've seen Lucy drunk in here I don't think she'd want to let it pass without comment. And he raises a toast to me. To the rest of my life. And the boys get out this cava and spray it all over me, and stick this stupid bloody crown on my head, and say they reckon Lucy would have wanted to join in with that and all. Then Bill gives me this tankard, look. For a present. Look. "To John, from his friends in the village." And I just cried. I couldn't help it.

LIZ   That's lovely. I think that's lovely.

JOHN   I thought they were keeping away. To show what they thought about things.

LIZ   Of course they weren't keeping away. You will have been loved by people here, John, you know all that stuff you were spouting this morning was bollocks. You will have been loved.

JOHN   I thought I'd let them down, is all.

She goes to him.

LIZ   You haven't done anything like that. You've done what you must. That's all right. People understand that. *(JOHN cries.)* Hey, hey. Don't cry. OK. Come here. Don't cry. Come on. *(a silence while JOHN recovers himself)* Well. It must have been a funny note to strike at a wake.

JOHN   I suppose so. I might have one more drink, d'you want one?

LIZ   Not for me, thanks, no.

JOHN   Fair enough. *(He starts looking for a bottle.)* It felt sort of good, though, really. When you thought about things. To raise a glass to something. Because she was lovely, you know? Did you know her?

LIZ   No.

JOHN I'd have thought she was in your choir. She was a good singer.

LIZ We don't have a choir, John. Shows how often you go to church.

JOHN Last time I went there was a choir.

LIZ That was a concert. I was sitting in front of you, that was some students singing *Acis and Galatea*, that wasn't a choir.

JOHN I don't know the difference really. It's all singing, innit. Her mum and dad were both there, I think they were happy when Bill stood up. Take the attention away, you know? Everyone looking at them and no one knowing what to say. It's such a sad thing, but she was lovely, so it felt sort of good to smile about something.

LIZ To be a bit happy.

JOHN Only because she always seemed happy.

LIZ I know.

JOHN When you're the bright one or the beautiful one in a place as small as this it stands out, you know? You matter to everyone. In towns, even if you're a genius, you're only ever really a drop in the ocean. We were all proud of her here. Even me, even us outsiders.

LIZ You weren't an outsider, you were the life and soul of the place.

JOHN For a little while, yeah.

He has found several beer bottles, but all of them are empty.

Fucking hell, I thought I'd brought enough to last me a while.

LIZ How long have you been out here?

JOHN Dunno. A while. That's probably why – oh, yeah. I'm so fucking hot, you know?

He takes off his shirt.

LIZ Oh, John.

JOHN Sweating like a fat lad.

He lies back, and spots another bottle.

LIZ Look at you.

JOHN This one isn't finished though.

LIZ Don't drink it, John.

She tries to take it off him.

JOHN What?

LIZ You've had enough, haven't you.

JOHN Have I?

LIZ I think you've had enough.

JOHN *gets up.*

JOHN Right. OK. I see. Don't go calling me a fuckin' alkie, yeah?

LIZ I'm not, I promise.

JOHN *leaps onto the bench.*

JOHN Cos people get shocked with how much I drink, but I'm all right, you know? I drink two litres of water at bedtime. My kidneys are fine. I got 'em checked. I don't get the shakes. I can handle my drink.

He leaps off the bench past **LIZ**.

LIZ All right.

JOHN And if you're thinking this is the classic aggressive behaviour of the alcoholic in denial, you can fuck yourself an' all, yeah?

He leaps onto the picnic bench.

HEY STELLA!!!

LIZ *laughs.*

Good right? Dead ringer, aren't I.

LIZ For the later Marlon Brando, maybe.

JOHN That's nice. Marlon Brando got invited to a fancy dress party—

LIZ Yeah?

JOHN Put a sheet over himself and went as Alaska. Boom boom!

LIZ Funny!

JOHN My brother's addicted to brake fluid, but he says he can stop at any time. Boom boom! Man walks into a bar, asks the barmaid for an innuendo, so she gives him one. Boom boom! This cafe had a sign in the window advertising breakfast at any time, so I went in and asked for French toast during the Renaissance!

LIZ *laughs again.*

I like your laugh.

LIZ Thank you.

JOHN I'm pleased you liked my jokes.

LIZ I sort of felt carpet-bombed into submission.

JOHN I think they call it clusterfucking.

LIZ Sounds exhausting.

JOHN   Boom boom. Christ, I'm out of breath. Strenuous brilliance, that's what tires me out.

LIZ   All right?

JOHN   Yeah, yeah.

LIZ   So you're actually selling tonight then are you? This is actually it, your last evening? And the man's turning up for the keys tomorrow morning?

JOHN   That's it.

LIZ   God.

JOHN   Weird, innit.

LIZ   I'm so gutted.

JOHN   Why?

LIZ   I don't know. I'm just sad.

JOHN   Gonna miss me?

LIZ   Oh, John.

JOHN   Sad for me you mean.

LIZ   For you, but... I don't know. I've felt like we were getting to know each other, you know? In the time I've been coming here. And I've enjoyed how that's been taking its time, cos I thought we were going to be doing this for years, I thought there was lots of time to, to take. I thought there was loads of chat to look forward to. But you're off.

JOHN   Right. Well.

LIZ   You'll definitely go?

JOHN   Yeah.

LIZ D'you know where yet?

JOHN No.

LIZ Mm.

JOHN What?

LIZ Could you not stay here? And still be part of it?

JOHN In the village?

LIZ Yeah.

JOHN I don't think I could go and pay for my drinks in there. And what would I do for work anyway? All fucking horrible jobs everyone does round here to make ends meet. I dunno why you trek all the way over here to do what you do, it's not so special really.

LIZ There's just nowhere any nearer home I can get a gig playing the organ. I'm not very good, to be honest, and all the places nearer by, they don't want me. It's a crappy little organ here. I think they might have scrapped it by now if I didn't keep turning up. Twenty quid in petrol money's all they can give.

JOHN How much does the petrol cost for the drive?

LIZ Twenty five quid.

JOHN That's good. That's very neat.

LIZ Yeah, I know.

JOHN Bit colder only wearing a vest.

LIZ I bet. So this is your last night.

JOHN Yeah.

LIZ What will you do with it?

JOHN I dunno. Probably cry into this funny little tankard.

LIZ Well that sounds fun.

JOHN Not to be missed. Why do you do it? The organ playing.

LIZ Well it's fun, isn't it. And it's only once a month, with the way the services work out.

JOHN No, but why do you actually do it?

LIZ What do you mean?

JOHN Why this and not watercolour painting? Or dogging or whatever.

LIZ I guess because I believe in it.

JOHN In God?

LIZ No, you don't have to believe in God to be an Anglican. That's the whole point. The right to have an equivocal relationship with everything, that's the point. I mean the ritual. And the songs. Some of them are really good songs. It's what we're all brought up with, isn't it. It's where we're all from. I think you have to pay some heed to that. Or someone does. Or I do, anyway.

JOHN I'm sure people are grateful that you do.

LIZ I'm sure they're not, I'm sure it never crosses their mind. But if – well imagine that who we are is the sum total of everything that's ever happened to us, right?

JOHN Right.

LIZ Well if that's true, if that was true, then I think old ceremonies must be important, because of that. And the church. The church is big, you know? Big thing. It's part of the reason for almost everything that's happened, isn't it. Cos it's in us, isn't it. Part of. Even the Beatles went to Sunday school, you know?

JOHN Sure.

LIZ And people say the church doesn't matter any more. And I think those people can sod off, to be honest, because it makes me so angry to hear someone dismiss another person's culture. And it's bollocks and all. Because it's still who we are, even if we ignore it. And I'm not saying it's a good thing or a bad thing, it's just a fact, it's who we are.

JOHN As long as you don't think it's an unbridled joy, I can go along with that.

LIZ No, no. It does terrible bloody damage, the church. But you fix things by getting to the cause, not burying it. And now Rowan Williams tells me we live in a post-Christian society and I think, hang on a minute. Because that's my culture you're attacking, and seeing as you were running the fucking joint a year ago, it really ought to be yours to defend as well. And who the hell are all the bishops sitting unelected in the Lords if we live in a post-Christian culture anyway? It's not the truth because look what the Queen's in charge of. He's probably just being paid to run the thing down cos someone wants to buy it.

JOHN What's your favourite hymn then?

LIZ What?

JOHN Go on, you must have a favourite.

LIZ No!

JOHN Any hymn.

LIZ "Praise my Soul The King of Heaven" then, I like that. Oh no, "Abide With Me. Abide With Me". They're by the same guy, you know.

JOHN Yeah?

LIZ Henry Francis Lyte. Isn't that a lovely name? Actually
there's a beautiful story about "Abide With Me".

JOHN Go on.

LIZ Well Lyte was the curate of All Saints Church in Brixham,
in Devon. By the sea. And he'd got ill, right? TB. And it was
decided he should move to Italy. For his health, they used
to think that helped, the climate and whatever. And after
he preached for the last time in his church, he'd been there
for twenty-seven years, he preached for the last time, and
when he was done he went down to the sea. It's like Matthew
Arnold, it's like *Dover Beach*. Ah love, let us be true to one
another, you know? And while he was on the beach, he
had this moment of, I don't know, this inspiration. And he
wrote "Abide With Me". And two weeks later he was dead.

JOHN No way.

LIZ Died in Nice on the way down to Italy. But the lovely thing,
right, the lovely thing is that you can go down to Brixham
and at eight every evening when the light's going out of the
sky, in summer anyway, it's dark in the winter of course,
but at the same time every evening they play the tune on
the church bells. Isn't that lovely?

JOHN That's lovely. Yeah. Have you been then?

LIZ No. I wanna go. I just haven't got round to it yet. They did it
at the funeral, "Abide With Me". That was one of the hymns.

JOHN Oh yeah?

LIZ Actually I don't like "Abide With Me" best.

JOHN No?

LIZ No. If I have to pick one, if I have to pick one it has to be
"Dear Lord and Father of Mankind".

JOHN That's a good one.

LIZ You know it?

> JOHN *sings the first verse of "**DEAR LORD AND FATHER OF MANKIND**", and* LIZ *joins in and sings it with him.*

Isn't that lovely?

JOHN Yeah, that's a good one. You know your organ playing?

LIZ What?

JOHN Your organ playing.

LIZ What about it?

JOHN Well—

LIZ Go on.

JOHN Well sometimes I think when I hear people talking a lot, what they're actually trying to do is not say what's really on their mind. What's actually getting to them.

LIZ Oh.

JOHN I was listening to you. Been listening. 'Bout keeping cultures alive or whatever. And I just don't buy it, really. I don't think people act out of such – cos I think you're not happy, Liz. That's what I think. And I don't think anything happens that isn't about feeling love or lack of love for another person, which might just be me, but that's what I think, so all the time I've been listening to you talk I've been getting this picture. Of a man you don't know any more you wish you still knew. I believe in that much more as an explanation for who you are than the one you've just given me. You mustn't mind me saying this. It's my last day, I want to be honest with you.

LIZ Right.

JOHN Am I wrong?

LIZ You're telling your own story, John, not mine, that's all.

JOHN My assessment of you—

LIZ Go on.

JOHN My assessment of you has always basically been that you're someone who needs to get laid.

LIZ Excuse me?

JOHN Don't you think? I think there's a sexual element in everything, I think that's what it is. I think everything is sex.

LIZ That's very definitely your story, not mine.

JOHN Maybe. But that's how I see you.

LIZ Well you can fuck off then, John.

JOHN What?

LIZ You div.

JOHN All I'm / trying to say—

LIZ I was being nice. I was trying to distract you, that's all. From how you were feeling, and you can fuck off do I need to get laid. Of course I need to get laid, don't we all, that's not who I bloody am!

JOHN Right.

LIZ God's sake!

JOHN Sorry.

LIZ Don't bother, all right? Fuck's sake.

JOHN I'm sorry. All I was trying to say was that I wanted to kiss you.

LIZ Right. I see. I'm going to go now.

JOHN Oh. / You don't—

LIZ I was only trying to be nice. I suppose you're unstable because of your wife.

JOHN I'm not—

LIZ You're such a fucking idiot. I've so liked talking to you, out here, our little chats, I've always looked forward to them. Never expecting anything to – come of it, that was what was so – because you had a wife, you were someone I could just talk to, you were finally someone to talk to. But you don't have a wife. Do you. And here I am. All you had to do was not fuck it up, John, because I've thought the world of you all the time I've been driving out here. And now you've fucked it up. There you go. That's that. I'm going to go.

JOHN Liz.

LIZ I have to go. Good bye. I – good bye.

JOHN Liz—

> **LIZ** *exits.* **JOHN** *sits alone. He hears someone coming.*
>
> *Enter* **MARK**.

MARK All right.

JOHN All right.

> **MARK** *puts his toolkit down.*
>
> You done then?
>
> *Silence.*

MARK I just thought I'd get more time with her than that.

Silence.

How was the—?

MARK *sits.*

Was that that funny woman from the church?

JOHN Leave it, will you, Mark? Let it remain as a beautiful snowflake.

ACT THREE

MARK *is wearing a suit. He has a fag. Enter* LIZ, *also dressed smartly.*

LIZ I know you, don't I?

MARK 'Scuse me?

LIZ Haven't we met before?

MARK Last year. I—

LIZ That's it.

MARK You're the organist.

LIZ That's me. Liz.

MARK Mark.

LIZ Yes. Hello again, Mark. Isn't it a beautiful day?

MARK Yeah.

LIZ This is a lovely village in the sun.

MARK Yeah.

LIZ I'm excited, seeing it on a Saturday. I don't usually come up here Saturdays, but there's a wedding.

MARK Yeah.

LIZ It's your wedding?

MARK Yeah.

LIZ Congratulations! That's lovely. That's so lovely. How are you feeling?

MARK Yeah. I mean. It's pretty—

LIZ It's the same for everyone, don't worry. I've done a lot of weddings. All the grooms I see, it's a big day.

MARK Yeah.

LIZ A happy day, but you get scared as well.

MARK Exactly.

LIZ Because in theory, this is the last person you'll ever shag, isn't it. And I know for a man that's quite—

MARK I'm not worried about that.

LIZ No? Well that's good then.

MARK Yeah.

LIZ Just the bloody magnitude of it.

MARK Loads of things. I, erm... Actually. I don't know whether I can do it, actually.

LIZ Oh.

MARK I just don't know – I don't know if it's gonna happen.

LIZ Oh right.

MARK I just thought I'd hide for a minute, you know, just—

LIZ Right. That's why you're—

MARK No one really comes round here, yeah. It's a bit like. Horrible. I don't know—

LIZ Do you want me to / leave you alone?

MARK No, no, it might be good to have someone to – I'm just scared, you know? Really – it's so weird like. And I can't talk to any of my mates, I can't.

LIZ What's up?

MARK It feels quite fast, you know? It feels quite fast. And I don't want to make a mistake. Cos I'd hurt her, if I was, and I couldn't bear it, you know? Cos she's amazing. I love her, you know? Only it feels quite fast.

LIZ When did you meet?

MARK Years back. School, like. She was below me in school. I sort of knew her, not properly but. But we started seeing each other like, nine months ago.

LIZ OK. That's not so fast if everything's wonderful?

MARK Yeah, and everything is, everything is wonderful. But I feel so lucky, you know? I can't believe my luck, that someone wanted me. So I feel like I'm pushing my luck. This. And I didn't think this would ever, ever happen to me, and it's now it's fucking happening today, and you're like – fuck.

LIZ Right, yeah.

MARK So that's it really.

LIZ Right. What are you gonna do?

MARK I dunno. My head's like...

LIZ Yeah.

MARK I keep thinking about all the things I thought I'd have done before I got married.

LIZ Oh yeah?

MARK Not big things. I don't mind not having done them, even. I never had a proper plan or...just – you know. I don't think I ever thought it was the sort of thing that – it's so real, isn't it.

LIZ What was it that you wanted to do? Before you got married, I mean.

MARK Well nothing big or anything. I haven't been to Wembley yet.

LIZ That's quite big.

MARK I wanted to have filled the bookshelf in my room.

LIZ What with?

MARK Books.

LIZ Yeah, what books?

MARK Oh, anything really. I'm not picky. Anything I could get in Sue Ryder. There's better stuff in charity shops than you'd think.

LIZ And was there anything else you thought you'd have done?

MARK I was going to see the world.

LIZ But you haven't?

MARK Not really. I had a bit of a disastrous attempt. I was going with a friend, round the world, you know, I was going to go travelling. This was years ago, this was when I was a teenager. Really looking forward to it. But they changed their mind about going with me, went round the world with someone else, my friend did.

LIZ Nice.

MARK Yeah. So I went on my own. And I spent about a week in India and it was just horrible, really, so I came home.

LIZ Oh.

MARK Yeah.

LIZ And you'd planned to stay out longer?

MARK Like six months, yeah.

LIZ Well six months is a lot of time to spend on your own.

MARK Yeah. I sometimes wish I'd stayed out there.

LIZ Yeah?

MARK Well I didn't get any refunds so it cost the same going for a week as it would have done going for half a year. More or less. What with the extra flights and all. And I'd quit my job and they wouldn't give it back so—

LIZ That's a shame.

MARK And I did – I felt I'd failed a bit. And I do feel like I haven't lived now, now that I'm settling down here properly. Haven't really tested myself or anything.

LIZ What was so horrible about India, do you mind me asking?

MARK Oh, it's hard to explain. I saw a dog tear a cat in two.

LIZ Right.

MARK Creep up on it and shake it till it came apart. I saw this child, this naked child squatting down to take a shit on a big pile of other people's shit, and these school children passing just spat at it. And the little kid looked so ashamed.

LIZ God.

MARK And the beggars. Guys with their eyes gouged out, you know? And sewed back up. These little girls would come up and ask me to buy them powdered milk for their baby brothers, then take you in a shop and you'd get charged like twenty quid for a packet. And I knew it was a stitch-up but I just had to do it cos when you go out at night, there are literally hundreds of people just lying down in the road to sleep. I spent about three hundred quid on powdered milk, just in the one week. Thought I deserved it. I just thought, you cunt. Coming over here like it's an adventure. When it's these people's lives. You don't know a fucking thing about anything. You deserve to be taken for all you've got. That was my attempt at widening my horizons. That was that. I thought it was so disrespectful to be there like I was. Just staring at everything. So all the money I didn't spend on powdered milk I took into Thomas Cook, this beautiful Thomas Cook with beautiful air conditioning, and I spent all the money I had on a plane ticket home.

LIZ You really didn't like it then.

MARK I hated myself for being there. I was an extra in a Bollywood movie. But yeah. That was that, anyway. Yeah.

LIZ And this friend who didn't go with you, that was your friend who died, was it?

MARK What?

LIZ I just thought you might be thinking of her, today. If she meant things to you.

MARK Right. Yeah. God, do you remember that?

LIZ Of course.

MARK Right, yeah, of course. It is a bit quick, isn't it.

LIZ I don't know.

MARK No?

LIZ Well it depends on how you feel, doesn't it.

MARK I suppose so.

LIZ It was a suicide, wasn't it, her death.

MARK What?

LIZ I thought it was a suicide.

MARK No one ever said anything like that.

LIZ Oh, I'm sorry.

MARK She just hadn't driven her car for a year. She'd had a few drinks and she wasn't used to driving and she was going a bit fast and she lost control.

LIZ How sad.

MARK It wasn't a suicide.

LIZ No, no.

MARK Did someone tell you that?

LIZ No! I'm just misremembering. I never quite knew the facts of the thing, and she was a student, wasn't she, and a lot of the time it's students who – and all I remembered was that she drove into the war memorial. I remember that, that phrase. And I'm just getting confused by language, I see it now. Because "drove" seems like such a deliberate word, doesn't it? But of course it doesn't have to mean she did it deliberately.

MARK It just means she was driving. She didn't do it on purpose.

LIZ No. That's good then. I mean, not good, sad. But better than – you know.

MARK Yeah. Anyway. Yeah.

The sound of singing from the front of the pub. They listen for a moment.

I never thought anyone would ever actually love me. And I think someone does. And I fucking love them. And I'm so scared of fucking it up because it's all come too soon after – yeah. You know what I mean.

LIZ Of course. Well maybe you're being sensible. Maybe you're right. Or maybe you just have to suck it and see, you know? People start early at a wedding, don't they! Is the party afterwards here as well?

MARK We'll end up here in the evening I reckon. We're going to the big house for the meal, like, the lunch. Place on your left when you drive in?

LIZ There's a wall and a big gate?

MARK The house is sort of behind a lot of trees, yeah. That's the main place here. And we're both from here, me and my – Rhiannon—

LIZ "My wife and I"!

MARK Yeah. So we hired the lawn and we've got a marquee. They've done us a deal.

LIZ And the weather's fine, so you've been lucky. Someone's smiling on this one!

MARK I hope so.

LIZ So it's a big old stately home, behind the wall.

MARK Well, sort of. The actual house is only really fifteen years old.

LIZ Oh?

MARK There used to be a big house there before. Local MP lived in it. Nice enough bloke. Not sure about his politics.

Anyway, one night there was this fire. Someone left a hob on or something, I don't know. And the whole place went up, and sort of collapsed in on itself. And the fire was so strong, so fierce, they never even found the bodies. The people who lived in the house. Whole family gone.

LIZ God.

MARK Yeah. After they'd finished with it as a crime scene, or whatever, the site got sold, and this property developer bought it. He'd made his money building blocks of flats in Bristol, and he wanted a place to live, so he rebuilt the house. Room for room, brick for brick, used the original plans, he lives there now with his family.

LIZ And does he have anything to do with everyone?

MARK Bloke like him doesn't have much to say to farmers.

LIZ Thought not. What sort of farmers live round here, do they do sheep?

MARK Some sheep, yeah.

LIZ I like sheep. Some people say cows are nicer but I think they kill people who walk their dogs. One day all these villages will be for rich people who commute into towns, I think. Sad.

MARK Way it goes, I think.

LIZ There must be books and books about it. The disappearing everything. Do you have those sorts of books on your shelf?

MARK It's more spy novels really.

LIZ Fair enough. I love a history book, me. The book I always think I'd like to read when I drive up over the chase is a history of road laying.

MARK A history of road laying?

LIZ No, it would be interesting! I'd love to know what everyone thought when all this tarmac started happening everywhere. Because that must have been such a shock to the psyche. Of the whole country. All those dirt tracks or whatever getting inked in for ever. It's like – it's like your war memorial isn't it.

MARK My war memorial?

LIZ The one you fixed. People live and die in villages like this all the time, don't they, and bit by bit the population of a village will change completely without anyone really noticing it. But write some deaths into stone, you can't help but look at how a place has changed, can you.

MARK Yeah.

LIZ It's the same with roads, I think. For as long as roads were really just places where enough people had walked to make a track, there must always have been a suspicion that they were invented, right? Like a dream. That enough people walking in a different direction could change the way a road went. But then you put down tarmac, and things are fixed for ever.

MARK I suppose that might be an interesting book.

LIZ I'm full of good ideas, me. I can always think of interesting books I could have written if only I'd been living at the right time. The trouble is we don't seem to be living through anything right now.

MARK No?

LIZ No, not really. I just mean it's hard to get things right while they happen to you, isn't it. To see, clearly. That's what I think anyway. You're going to be my last gig here, you know.

MARK Really?

LIZ I have to stop doing it. Playing here, I mean. The organ. I'm pleased it's you who's getting married, it's nice that it's someone I know.

MARK I'm gonna go through with it then, am I?

LIZ I was hoping I might be able to slip that in without you noticing.

MARK No, I'm a sharp tack, I am.

LIZ What about you, will you stay round here once you're married?

MARK Oh, yeah. I work in there now, anyway, so.

LIZ I didn't know that! God have I said anything rude about it? Only I do think the sexual politics of the calendars hanging in the loos are quite problematic, and sometimes I blurt things out.

MARK No, you're all right.

LIZ Thank God.

MARK What's wrong with the calendars in the loos? It's just the local hunt doing *Calendar Girls*, it's all for charity.

LIZ Yes, but you've had it open on the same month for about a year now, and I had a flick through and it's definitely because the girls from May 2013 have got the nicest arses.

MARK Oh, yeah, they have. Is that bad?

LIZ It is a bit bad, I think.

MARK Sorry.

LIZ Well, just something to think about maybe. So where are you at in your head? What are you going to do, d'you think?

MARK Oh, God. I feel like if I just stay here, and never make a decision, maybe that'll be OK.

LIZ Do you think?

MARK I don't think I can.

LIZ No?

MARK It won't work. I won't be able to – I'll let her down. Fuck's sake. I don't feel like I can. How come you're stopping playing the organ? You said I was your last gig.

LIZ Oh, lots of reasons. The organ's shot, for one thing, and they'll never afford to replace it.

MARK No?

LIZ Organs are expensive. And I don't know whether they should be much of a priority these days for churches.

MARK Why not?

LIZ I sort of think raising funds to help poor people or the elderly or whatever might be more important, you know? Is this what you want to be talking about, is this—

MARK All I want to do is not talk about that. Just for a little bit longer.

LIZ OK.

MARK So will you tell me something else? Anything else. About why they shouldn't fix the organ, or whatever, I don't care, I'm not really listening, I just don't want to think.

LIZ Sure. OK. Well, I don't think they ought to renew the organ because you know, music changes as well, you know. And God knows, it's my culture, and even a year ago I thought it was all worth saving. But the world changes, doesn't it.

MARK It does.

LIZ And if people want drum kits in church perhaps they should be allowed them. I'm talking too much about organs. You must need to get back to your people.

MARK No, they know I wanted a minute.

LIZ I think what I feel very conscious of is the fact that everything comes to an end, you see. A time always comes when it's time to move on. When I started coming here I was in quite a sad place, actually. Quite a sad bloody place. So I was looking for things to do, so I could drown out my spare time. And these days I feel much better about all that, so I don't think I need all the driving here and back as much.

MARK What do you do for a living?

LIZ I teach piano.

Enter JOHN.

JOHN Hands off cocks, on socks!

LIZ Oh.

MARK Fucking hell, hello John!

JOHN All right mate, how's tricks?

MARK Good man, yeah. It's so good to see you!

JOHN Course it is.

MARK I didn't know whether you'd got your invitation.

JOHN No?

MARK You didn't reply to it.

JOHN No?

MARK I don't know whether there's a seat for you at lunch.

JOHN Ah well. 'My bad', as the cool kids say. You'll be able to fit me in?

MARK I dunno mate, to be honest. It's all like—

JOHN I'll skip a course and come to the party. Sorry mate. Should have written back. Hello Liz, how are you?

He gives her a kiss on the cheek.

LIZ Hello John.

JOHN You look well.

LIZ Thank you. So do you.

JOHN Do I? Christ, imagine what I must have looked like when you saw me last. So you're having second thoughts are you?

MARK What?

JOHN Everyone knows, mate. Stands to reason. It's your wedding day and you're chain-smoking round the back of the pub. Aren't they sweet, the young? They think it's all happening for the first time.

LIZ Well it is for him.

JOHN That's true. Mark, I want you to listen to me.

MARK Right.

LIZ John—

JOHN It's all right. Mark. You have never believed you were worth much. But you always have been. You were shit at peeling potatoes when you used to work here, but everyone liked having you around. And you lost someone, very recently. But life goes on, mate. And here's someone standing with their hand out waiting for you. And you have to make a decision.

MARK Right.

JOHN Because things don't always happen at the pace we'd choose. So maybe this is all happening a little bit quickly. But that's life, isn't it. And I suppose you have to ask yourself this. Do you want to try? Or would you rather never risk anything?

MARK Right.

JOHN You see what I mean, don't you.

MARK Yeah.

JOHN Well don't be a cunt then.

MARK OK. Right. Yeah.

JOHN Probably time to get down the church an' all.

MARK Is it? Oh Christ. I'd better go.

JOHN Good man. Feel good?

MARK Yeah. Yeah. I feel good. Yeah. Thanks.

JOHN Fuck off then.

MARK Thanks Liz.

LIZ Are you all right?

MARK Yeah.

LIZ Are you going to be all right?

MARK Yeah. Yeah. I feel really good.

> **MARK** *exits.*

JOHN Sweet boy, isn't he.

LIZ He's so frightened.

JOHN So was I. Were you ever married?

LIZ Yeah.

JOHN What happened to your husband?

LIZ He died.

JOHN Oh, Liz.

LIZ Yeah. Congenital cardiomyopathy.

JOHN Fuck. I'm sorry.

LIZ Me too. It was years ago now though. I was very scared as well.

JOHN Yeah. I didn't know, Liz, I'm sorry.

LIZ You don't have anything to apologise for. I ought to get down the church if he's headed that way. It'd be typical me if the bride came up the aisle and I was still puffing my way up the hill. It's nice to see you.

JOHN I hoped I'd see you.

LIZ Oh yeah?

JOHN Yeah.

LIZ Well. We're lucky then, aren't we.

JOHN Yeah, I guess we are.

LIZ I'd better make a start.

JOHN Sure, of course. See you later maybe.

LIZ OK.

JOHN Bye then.

LIZ Bye, John. Bye.

   LIZ *exits.*

ACT FOUR

The evening of the wedding. Sound of a good night from the front of the pub. JOHN *is sitting with a pint, staring into it. Enter* MARK, *lighting up.*

MARK So this is where you're hiding.

JOHN I didn't know you smoked.

MARK You all right?

JOHN What?

MARK Are you all right?

JOHN Oh, you know me.

MARK What does that mean?

JOHN I'm all right.

MARK All right.

JOHN Yeah. So have you got my job here, then? Someone told me this is your gaffe now.

MARK No, erm, assistant manager.

JOHN Fuck off.

MARK Yeah, not just a pretty face.

JOHN What does a pub need an assistant manager for?

MARK Yeah, yeah. It's all the same work. We just have different titles.

JOHN I bet you've got a microwave.

MARK What?

JOHN I bet you've got a microwave.

MARK Yeah.

JOHN There you go. Not all the same, is it. I wouldn't have let one of those through the door. But everything slides under capitalism, dunnit. Anyway. Good show this afternoon.

MARK Yeah, it was all right, wasn't it.

JOHN Felt good doing it?

MARK Fucking amazing actually.

JOHN Yeah?

MARK Really like – sure of it. Yeah. Certain. What the fuck is all this? Someone's kicked the hose over. It was probably you.

JOHN Probably.

The boys in the pub start singing football songs.

Listen to that. Pissheads.

MARK Yeah.

JOHN Not often you get everyone you care about in the same room, is it.

MARK No, it's cool.

JOHN Good things, weddings. Break up the slog.

MARK Yeah.

MARK *starts sorting out the hose.*

JOHN Want a hand?

MARK You're all right.

JOHN Go on, we can start at different ends. It'll be like *Lady and the Tramp*.

MARK All right.

JOHN I'm glad you're working here though, that's good news. Bit of continuity. Nice to know they haven't just shipped in a bunch of Poles from Andover, you know?

MARK We haven't got any Poles, no.

JOHN Not that there'd be anything wrong with that, of course.

MARK We've got a Slovenian girl.

JOHN Oh yeah?

MARK She's nice. She's gonna be an interior designer. And we've got two Filipino brothers called Joey and Ken. Well, those aren't their real names. They changed them when they came over to sound more English.

JOHN What were their names before?

MARK Joey's name was Irisjim.

JOHN Yeah, the locals'd laugh at that.

MARK Ken's funnier though. You'll like Ken's.

JOHN Why?

MARK His real name was Edward.

JOHN That's brilliant.

MARK Changed it from Edward to Ken to sound more English. They picked the new ones out of *Friends* and *Barbie*.

JOHN Is that what passes for English culture in the Philippines?

MARK They might have been spinning me a yarn. They're funny boys. Quicker than me anyway. They're both training as accountants. In Bournemouth.

JOHN Oh yeah?

MARK You've done your coils bigger than mine.

JOHN That's all right, isn't it?

MARK Guess so. Stick it by the table.

JOHN Don't you want it in the shed?

MARK They'll water the grass out front in the morning.

JOHN You water the grass?

MARK Yeah. It looks nicer.

JOHN But you water the fucking grass?

MARK It needs water, dunnit.

JOHN Things really have changed.

MARK There's nothing wrong with watering the grass.

JOHN No, no. I'm sure it's very neat and tidy.

MARK Yeah.

The boys in the pub are singing pop songs.

JOHN You were telling me about your Filipino mates.

MARK Yeah. Well. Nothing really to say about them. They're my mates. Yeah. I've learned a bit of Filipino so I can understand what they're talking about when it's just the three of us, on shift. *Pagod ako.* I'm tired. *Goutom ako.* I'm hungry. *Bogi ako.* I'm handsome. *Maganda ikao.* She's beautiful.

JOHN Little Rosetta Stone aren't you.

MARK I knew some other stuff but I forgot. Keeps me entertained on shift, trying to remember it all.

JOHN I guess you can't entertain yourself by drinking while you work any more.

MARK No, there's none of that. But we have a laugh. You've got to have a laugh, haven't you.

JOHN No you haven't.

MARK Oh.

JOHN That's what kids think. Fun. That's not how it goes. I'll tell you how it goes, Mark. You've got to work and then you've got to die.

MARK Oh.

JOHN And you've got to get married, of course.

MARK Yeah. That's quite fun.

JOHN You wait and see.

MARK Yeah, maybe.

JOHN You'll be all right, I reckon. Keep off the drink. Don't forget her birthday. And enjoy tonight. You going on holiday?

MARK Yeah. Bournemouth.

JOHN Bournemouth?

MARK Shit, sorry, no. Brighton.

JOHN I was gonna fucking say. Christ, Bournemouth. That'd be a short marriage.

MARK Right.

JOHN How long have you been working here then?

MARK 'Bout six months now I think.

JOHN Yeah? It's so weird to think you're married now.

MARK Why?

JOHN You're a little kid.

MARK Little married kid.

JOHN Christ.

MARK Yeah.

JOHN Where you living now?

MARK Well, that's the bad news. We're actually living in Andover.

JOHN Fuck off.

MARK Nothing we can afford round here.

JOHN That's a shame, mate, I'm sorry.

MARK It's not what we'd want, obviously. But you do what you must, don't you.

JOHN So you live in Andover and commute out here to work?

MARK That's it.

JOHN Fair enough.

MARK So how are you, anyway?

JOHN Pretty good, actually. I contacted a stockbroker I used to serve in here when I left, and he invested the money I got from my half of the pub in futures. And the portfolio's performed pretty well, and I'm actually a millionaire now.

MARK Seriously?

JOHN No, course not. But I'm all right. I haven't really decided what to do with the rest of my miserable life, yet, mind.

MARK Still?

JOHN It's only been a year.

MARK Yeah. All the same, John. Gotta enjoy it while it lasts, haven't you.

JOHN I've had bits and bobs of fun, don't worry. I've got all the money I got for her to spend, haven't I. Did a bit of travelling. The mountains of Nepal.

MARK What was that like?

JOHN It was all right. Mountains were nice. I'm not convinced about travelling though.

MARK No?

JOHN I don't know why all these eighteen-year-olds do it. The odd nice view, but you're basically always just looking for things to do, you know?

MARK Oh yeah?

JOHN Yeah. Cos there's no work, and there's only so many hours a day you can spend being fascinated by how foreign everything is. 'Specially at my age, when your ankles swell up. Still, kids like it, don't they.

MARK They do.

JOHN If I had a kid, I'd tell him not to bother. You get more out of getting on with something, I think, that's what I wish I could do. I just can't think of anything to get on with.

MARK That's cos you're not happy.

JOHN Yeah?

MARK A traveller, on his journey, changes only his skies and not his self.

JOHN Where's that from?

MARK Can't remember. Someone's Facebook cover photo. Some book I read in the loo.

JOHN You kept up the reading then?

MARK There isn't time really.

JOHN Can I ask you something?

MARK Go on.

JOHN I always thought you'd get out of here one day. What with all your books. Bright bloke that you are. Cos there's not much here for you, is there, unless you always wanted to be an assistant manager.

MARK Is that a question?

JOHN Well, are you planning on doing anything, is all I meant? Have you got a plan?

MARK I'm making one.

JOHN Right. Yeah.

MARK One foot in front of the other.

JOHN Yeah. Can I ask you something else?

MARK Don't ask me about her, John, will you?

JOHN I just / wondered how you were about—

MARK It's all in the past, yeah? It's all something I'm moving on from.

JOHN Probably a good thing. Probably good to keep trucking on.

MARK Yeah.

JOHN And you've found someone you love.

MARK Yeah, I have. And I married her. Cos I didn't see the point in living in the past John, in dreaming. Cos the brave thing people do is get on with it, you know? So I married her. And when I needed a job I found a job.

JOHN And heaven knows you're miserable now.

They laugh.

Isn't it funny how time just seems to happen to you? And you never really seem to do anything except go along with it.

MARK Oh, there are deliberate decisions you make along the way. I took up smoking.

JOHN Your Dad'd be proud.

MARK Yeah.

JOHN I stopped drinking.

MARK Did you?

JOHN No. But I drink much less cos I can't get it at cost any more.

MARK I bet. Do you wanna come and see in the kitchen, everything we've cocked up since you left?

JOHN *laughs.*

What?

JOHN I don't think so.

MARK No? Fair enough.

JOHN I had my life in there, you know? I slept in there for fifteen years. This was my life, here.

MARK OK.

JOHN Sorry. Nothing to do with you.

MARK It's not the same without you. No one's very good at jokes round here any more.

JOHN No?

MARK I don't know how you came up with all yours.

JOHN Joke books, mate. You didn't think I was making them all up, did you?

MARK Oh. I thought you did.

JOHN No, read joke books to keep me sane. Hm.

MARK I'd better go back really.

JOHN Course.

MARK It was really good of you to come. Meant a lot to have you there.

JOHN Wouldn't have missed it.

MARK You wanna come in with me?

JOHN In a minute, yeah. Everyone still comes in then, do they?

MARK Yeah. Apart from Bill Owen. You remember Bill?

JOHN Yeah?

MARK Dead.

JOHN Oh yeah.

MARK Apart from that everyone still comes in.

JOHN I hoped they'd stay away once I left. Not seriously. Not actually. I do know it's their pub. I just hoped a bit they might want to stick it to the man.

MARK I don't think they think of a pint as a political act.

JOHN Fair enough.

MARK You'll be all right, yeah, John? You'll find something you want to do soon.

JOHN Thanks, mate. Oh, I meant to ask.

MARK Yeah?

JOHN Liz. The organist. Have you seen her around? I wanted to talk to her.

MARK I think she's gone actually.

JOHN Oh.

MARK She said she had to head home.

JOHN Oh.

MARK Said she wouldn't have a drink cos she didn't like drinking and driving.

JOHN Oh. Would you know where I could look her up, by any chance?

MARK The church'll have her number?

JOHN Yeah. Good thought. The church. She seem all right when you last saw her?

MARK Yeah, she was all right.

JOHN Mm. I had it in mind to talk to her, about something. Something. But she's gone, has she?

MARK Yeah, she left after the service.

JOHN Well. Maybe if she's happy I'll leave it at that. Hey Mark.

MARK Yeah?

JOHN I bet the first thing you did when you started was block up that grate. You used to hate that, didn't you.

MARK No, the fire's still going.

JOHN Oh yeah?

MARK Yeah. It's like you said, that's what we're selling, really. Sweat and dogs.

JOHN Did I say that?

MARK Don't you remember?

JOHN I don't remember very much sometimes, Mark. I think I fucked my head.

MARK Don't be silly, mate.

JOHN No, I do, I think I drank myself stupid. Sometimes I don't remember much.

MARK John.

JOHN I'm all right. I'm happy today, this is a proper happy fucking day.

MARK You'll find things to do, John.

JOHN Yeah.

MARK I remember a lot of your little sayings. Think of you a lot.

JOHN Yeah?

MARK Bit of a mantra that, for me. Sweat and dogs. You taught me everything I know about market positioning.

JOHN Well that's some comfort I suppose. In your chain. You know, your—

MARK Yeah?

JOHN Well I was just thinking, they must have other pubs need running, right? You couldn't, like, ask the right person if they need an old landlord anywhere for me, could you?

MARK I think it's all apply online now.

JOHN Oh.

MARK They advertise it online and you upload your CV for central office, yeah.

JOHN Right.

MARK I don't really—

JOHN No, of course, stupid thought. Just. Nah, stupid.

MARK I can give you the web address? Get it on my phone, hang on. It'll be like / www.—

JOHN No, you're all right mate, sorry. That's not me. I'm moving on. That's not me. I'm gonna move on.

MARK You'll be all right.

JOHN Yeah.

> *The boys in the pub start singing **"ABIDE WITH ME".***
> **JOHN** *and* **MARK** *listen to them.*

Fuck, I'm a miserable bastard, aren't I. Sorry mate. You got fucking married!

MARK Yeah!

JOHN It's amazing, isn't it? You got your life right!

MARK Yeah. That's a nice way of...yeah. Day I left school I came here with Lucy. And we drank a bit and we started arguing, cos she wasn't going to leave her boyfriend, she was going out with this older guy and she told me she loved me but... And I started to get upset. Cos I knew even then, I knew it wasn't gonna happen. She was never going travelling with me. And I knew in five years' time we wouldn't know each other any more. And she stood on this bench and made me get up there with her. And she pointed at the big house and the view, and she said, look over there. See that? That's the world. That's where we're gonna go. We're gonna do everything. We're gonna have the most brilliant time. And when we get back to England we won't forget each other. Because we'll have shared the whole world, won't we. We're gonna live the best lives ever. We're gonna do everything we want. And I love what I have now. But I'm so glad I had that afternoon. Cos for an afternoon, I believed that. I got to believe that.

The lights go down.

End

PROPS LIST

ACT ONE
Onstage:
Firewood   (page 2)

Toolkit (**Mark**)   (page 1)
Log basket (**John**)   (page 1)
Cigarettes (**Liz** and **Mark**)   (page 11)
Three drinks (**John**)   (page 12)

ACT TWO
Onstage:
Bench
Beer bottles

Crown and pewter tankard with glass bottom (**John**) (Page 25)
Toolkit (**Mark**)   (page 37)

ACT THREE
Cigarette (**Mark**)   (page 39)

ACT FOUR
Onstage:
Hose

Pint (**John**)   (page 56)
Cigarette and lighter (**Mark**)   (page 56)

THIS IS NOT THE END

Lightning Source UK Ltd.
Milton Keynes UK
UKOW01f2331241017
311580UK00005B/37/P